Look, here they come! A blue jay pair.

They hop! They stop! They test the air.

They take their gifts—but hide them away.

They'll need them more on a winter's day.

Jaay! Jaay!

Carolina Wren

Little wrens roam
in search of home.

Tea-kettle!
Tea-kettle!

Car or box?

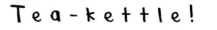

Tea-kettle!
Tea-kettle!

Cans or blocks?

Tea-kettle!
Tea-kettle!

Fern or nest?

Tea-kettle!

Tea-kettle!

Which one's best?

Common Redpoll

Zip! Zap!

Flip! Flap!

An acrobat with a crimson cap.

Peck! Inspect!

Knock! Collect!

A tiny bird of great intellect.

Chit chit chit!
Chit chit chit!
Chit chit chit!

Snow Bunting

Chi-tik! Chi-tik! Come quick! Come quick!

A flurry is hurrying through the air.

Twinkling lights in magical flight,

they'll land again soon—

but where?

Snow Goose

Snowflakes whirling,

snow-flocks swirling,

KREEY-A!!!!!!

ki-ki-ki-ki! ki-ki-ki-ki!

ki-ki-ki-ki! ki-ki-ki-ki!

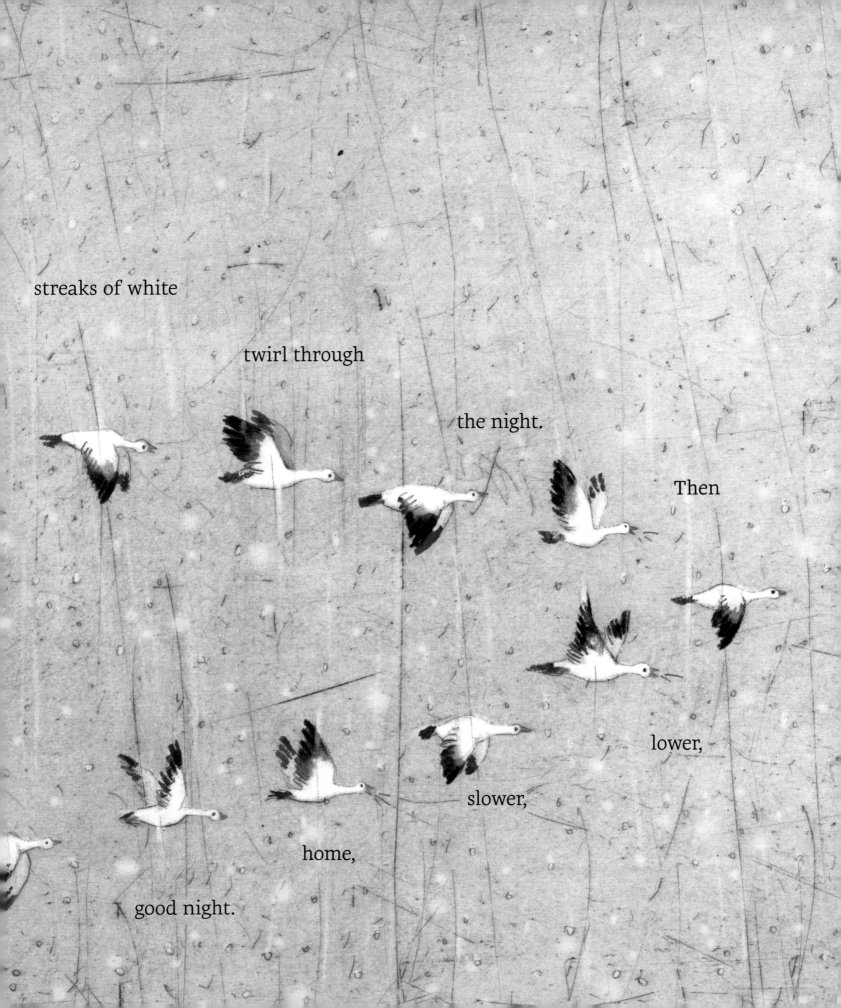

streaks of white

twirl through

the night.

Then

lower,

slower,

home,

good night.

Black Rosy-Finch

Hop! Stop! Hop! Stop!

SO MUCH SNOW!

Check! Peck! Check! Peck!

COME ON, LET'S GO!

Peep! Cheep! Peep! Cheep!

WE WANT MORE!

Till back they bounce

through the barn house door.

Atlantic Puffin

It starts with a splash!

bubble rings

It's gone in a flash!

beating wings

The sea parrot steers,

left and right.

Lower,

slower,

dimming light . . .

Danger! Danger! School's dismissed!

The puffin hunts the ones it missed.

SNATCH! CATCH! This battle of wills

will end with a flopping fish-filled bill.

Errrrrrrrrrrrrrrrrrrrrrrrr

Ivory Gull

Out of the blue

comes dinner for two.

(In such harsh conditions,

it's what they must do.)

Bohemian
Waxwing

and MORE!

and more,

and more,

then more,

then four,

then a few,

were two,

First there

Dark clouds winging,

taunting, singing,

the lawless flock

has come for the hawk.

The frightened raptor sits frozen still.

WILL THEY EVER LEAVE?

Yes,

they will!

(But for now, this hawk's fear

is their thrill.)

Sirrrrr sirrrrr sirrrrr!

Sirrrrr sirrrrr sirrrrr!

Great Gray Owl

Plunging from
her post . . .
a hook-billed
forest ghost!

Grrrrrrrrrrrrok!

(Did the hare escape? Almost.)

Ruffed Grouse

Beneath the snow lies a winter house.

A tunneled hole for a sleeping grouse.

It dreams of trembling aspen flowers—

breakfast in just a few short hours!

For now, sleep tight. Little grouse, keep warm.

You're safe in your white-walled winter dorm.

Quirt-quirt-quirt-quirt-quirt-quirt-quirt-quirt!

HOOT!

HOOT!

HOOT!

HOOT!

HOOT!

HOOT!

Snowy Owl

Up above, a crescent moon.

Down below, a crested dune.

In the air, a haunting tune.

Don't come near here anytime soon.

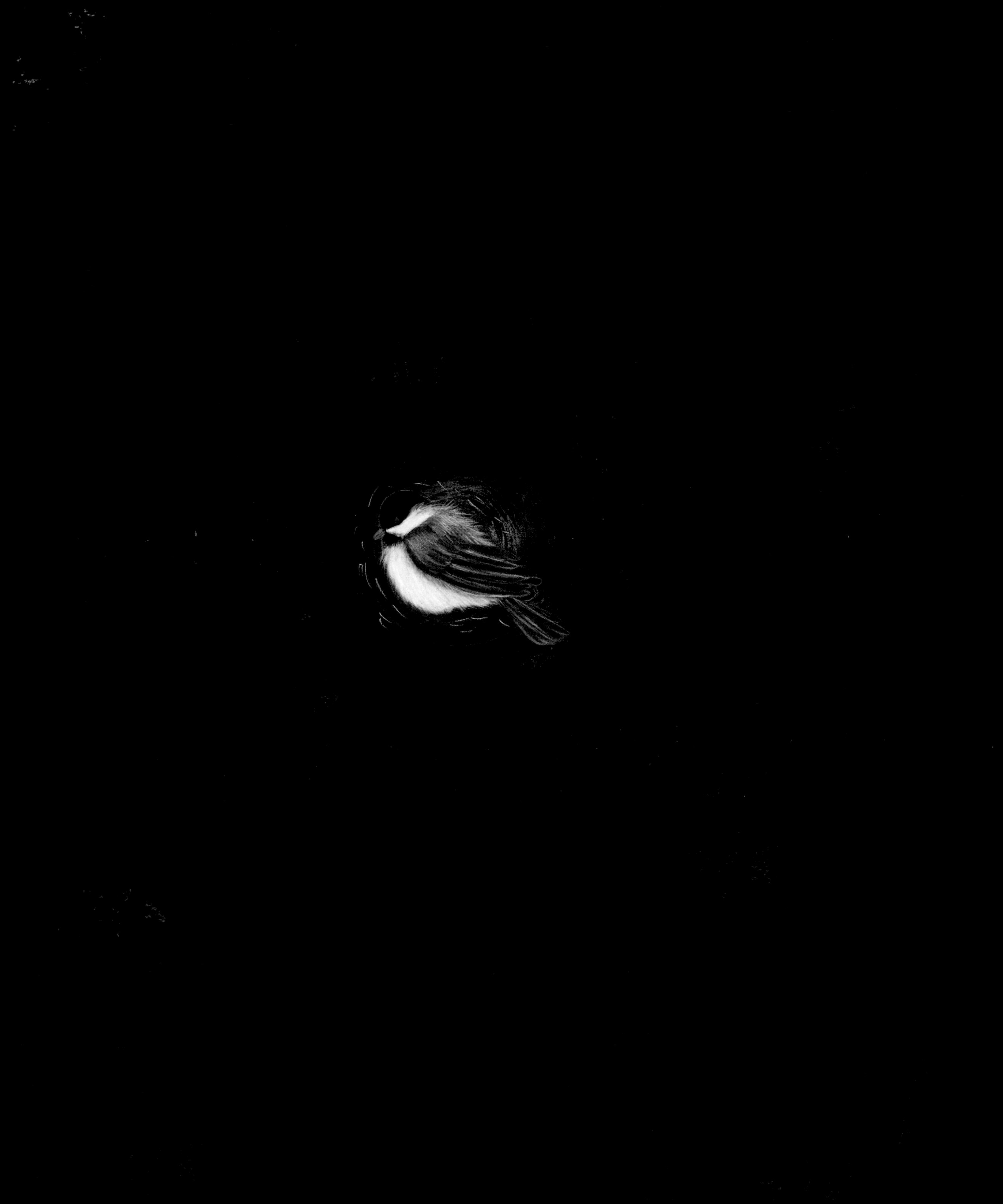

Black-Capped Chickadee

Shaking

quaking,

in a tree,

a stoic,

heroic

chickadee.

Fluffing,

puffing,

out of sight.

Heating,

beating

this winter night.

Fee-bee! Fee-bee!

Golden-Crowned Kinglet

Five little kings,
warriors with wings!
Each frigid night
means time to fight.
They find their fort—
a feathered court!—
then shiver and quiver,
each lending support.

American Tree Sparrow

Teedle-eet eet!

Teedle-eet eet!

Sparrows sing,

cool air rings

in tiny bell sounds.

Teely-wit wit!
Teely-wit wit!

Melting snow,

time to go!

Back to breeding grounds . . .

Downy Woodpecker

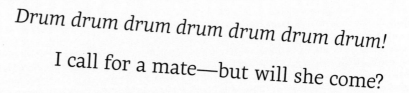

Peck peck peck peck peck peck peck peck!
Where are the insects? Let me check.

Drum drum drum drum drum drum drum!
I call for a mate—but will she come?

Drill drill drill drill drill drill drill!
I'm building a home for eggs to fill.

Knock knock knock knock knock knock!
It's here at last! It's spring o'clock!

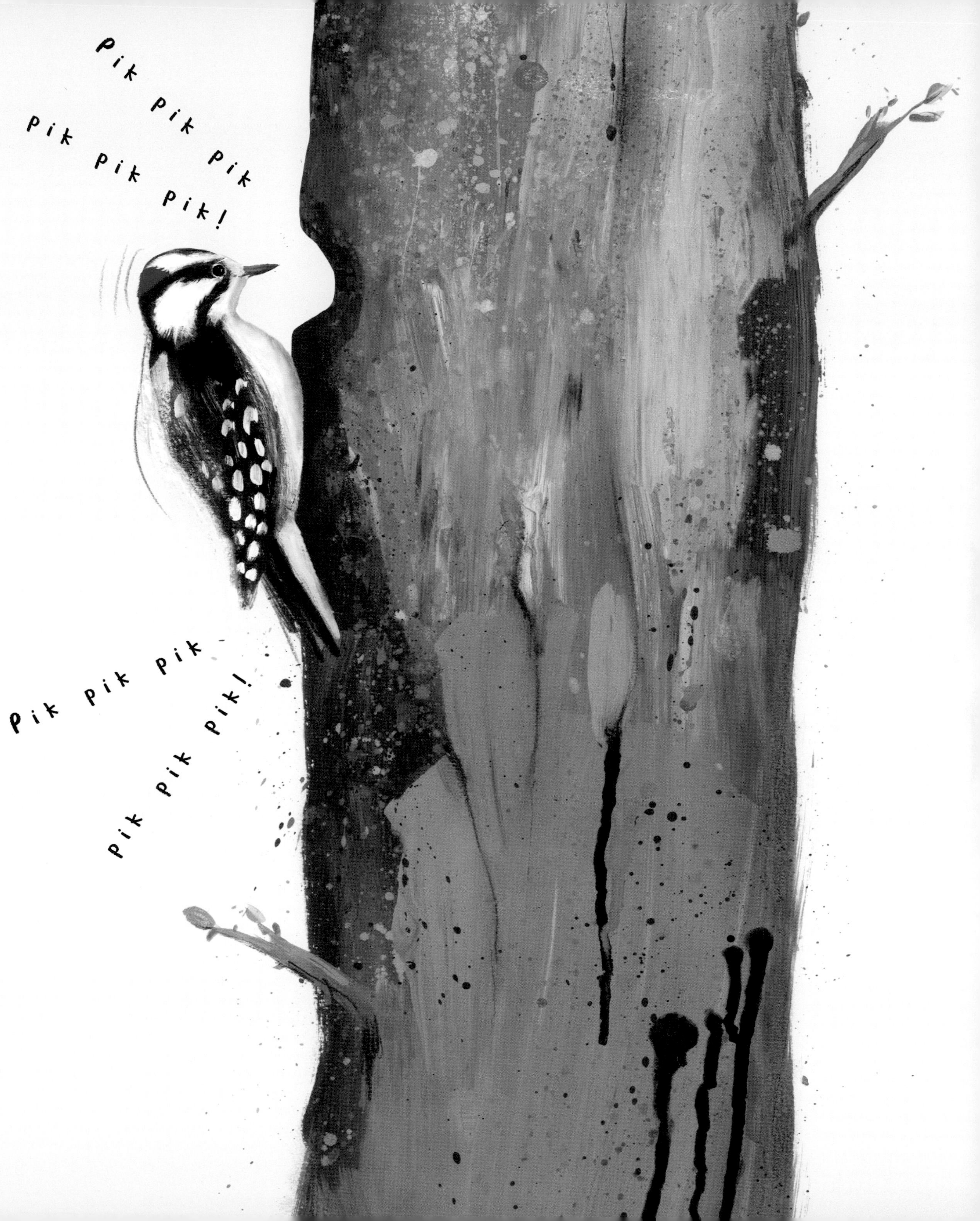
Pik pik pik
pik pik pik
pik!
Pik pik pik
pik pik pik!

Northern Cardinal

What-cheer,
cheer, cheer,
birdie-birdie-birdie!

What-*cheer-cheer-cheers* do the cardinals say?

Springtime is coming, it's weeks away!

Somewhere nearby flies a bumblebee queen!

Under this snowfall's a world of green!

Bushes are budding and bursting below!

A strong earthy scent lies beneath all that snow!

Butterflies waltz in the wind—let's cheer!

Signs all around us show springtime is near.

Jaay!
Jaay!
Jaay!

Blue Jay

Look! In the tree! A blue jay nest.

Sticks were gathered, twigs compressed.

See how she shaped them like a cup?

Home sweet home! *Click click!* Look up!

Look! In the sky! A second jay.

Bearing gifts, he's come to stay.

Mating, waiting, still just two—

But spring will bring more life anew.

MEET THE BIRDS!

Blue Jay

In fall's final days, the blue jay gathers and hides nuts and seeds—up to one hundred a day! Even a month later, the intelligent blue jay will remember its secret hiding spots, which may be as far as two and a half miles from where its food was first collected. Storing the food it finds away in advance helps the jay to survive incoming winter's harsher weather, a time when it becomes more difficult to find anything new to eat. As winter turns to spring, blue jays are busy. Males court females, sometimes in aerial chases and other times with edible treats. In pairs, blue jays will build nests together using twigs, bark strips, moss, weeds, and grass they both gather. Female jays will stay behind inside these cup-shaped nests to incubate eggs, while males will hunt for food and return with it. When new baby jays are born, they too will live inside these nests for almost a month.

Carolina Wren

The Carolina wren sometimes roosts and nests in trees. At other times, it makes its home inside mailboxes, tin cans, bird nesting boxes, planters, or even old coat pockets! The Carolina wren is one of the few wren varieties that do not migrate south during the winter. While they are not one of the hardiest of snow birds, they can survive most mild to moderate winter seasons.

Common Redpoll

The common redpoll eats up to 42 percent of its bodyweight in birch each day in the wintertime. The tiny acrobat zips and zooms between trees, knocking seeds to the ground, which it then swallows and stores inside a special throat pouch. Once safe and sound back in its nest, the redpoll will regurgitate the seeds and crack them open in order to eat them properly.

Snow Bunting

The snow bunting, also called the snowflake, is in constant motion between earth and sky. Landing when it spies a good spot to hunt, it crouches low to forage. But it won't stay down for long—just a few minutes later, it's right back up in the air! As snow buntings fly together, they create the illusion of a rolling wave, with the birds at the back continuously flying over and ahead of those at the front.

Snow Goose

Many snow geese migrate south in the wintertime—but not all. Some are left behind, bottled up due to bad weather. Flocks with families may also migrate more slowly than those without, as they need to stop to refuel more frequently during their travels. Winter flocks feed mostly on any waste grain they can find on farms and agricultural fields.

Black Rosy-Finch

The black rosy-finch hops about during the day—as if playing leapfrog!—while hunting in large flocks for food. It pecks at thin layers of snow on the ground, constantly searching for bugs and seeds. At nighttime, the finches roost together in enclosed spaces where they can stay warm. One common place to find them is huddled on rafters inside barns.

Atlantic Puffin

In the icy wintertime, the Atlantic puffin, also called the sea parrot, lives on the open sea. Its waterproof feathers help it to stay warm while it floats or swims underwater. It drinks saltwater, filtering out the salt through glands in its nostrils. To eat, the puffin dives deep down in the water, flapping its wings as if flying and steering with its feet. A typical dive will net ten fish. The puffin's tongue keeps its prey trapped inside its mouth even while it opens its beak to catch more.

Ivory Gull

The ivory gull is the ultimate winter survivor. While life on a polar desert or icy glacier would likely mean death for almost any other bird, the ivory gull has learned how to live in truly impossible conditions. It hunts around the clock, even in the dark of night. It walks in the wake of polar bears, eating what remains from their kills. It even feeds on the droppings of walruses and seals.

Bohemian Waxwing

The Bohemian waxwing spends its winters both in open woods—where it can roost in dense trees and hedges—and in towns with fruit trees. The waxwing roams in large flocks called ear-fulls, frequently descending on gardens and parks in search of berries. Enemies of the waxwing include buzzards, hawks, and falcons. The waxwing is safest—and can even be threatening!—when it stays with other waxwings in very large groups.

Great Gray Owl

The great gray owl lives and hunts deep within the coniferous forest. Its puffy feathers help to protect it from harsh weather conditions. With a keen sense of hearing, this owl can detect even a rodent's heartbeat as it tunnels beneath the snow's surface. When hunting, it perches in a tree, cocks its head to the side, and listens. Then, once it detects prey, it will swoop downward with noiseless wings, capturing its unsuspecting meal with its sharp talons.

Ruffed Grouse

The ruffed grouse adapts for winter in many ways. It grows new bristles and feathers, both on its feet and around its beak. It finds protection from cold winds in trees, often firs. And it snow roosts: First, it finds deep, powdery snow. Then it tunnels and burrows into it, building a nighttime shelter. Hidden from the outside world and possible predators, the grouse can finally slow its metabolism, burn less energy, and rest.

Snowy Owl

In wintertime, the snowy owl can be found along dunes and prairie marshes and in other open areas. Its light coloring helps to provide camouflage when perched on snow. Its dense, downy feathers keep its body much warmer than the air outside, even allowing it to sit comfortably for hours in temperatures as low as 40°F below zero. Solitary and territorial, the snowy owl will hoot—up to six times—when defending its space.

Black-Capped Chickadee

The black-capped chickadee has several ways of surviving winter. It carefully hides food. It grows a denser coat. And it finds cavities to roost in—snug spaces within the partially rotting wood of trees and stumps or even abandoned woodpecker holes. Before nighttime, the tiny birds stuff themselves full of as many seeds and frozen insects as they possibly can. Then they enter into a hypothermic state, shivering and lowering their body temperatures by as much as 22°F in order to conserve energy.

Golden-Crowned Kinglet

Only about one out of every six golden-crowned kinglets will live a full year. And winter can be an especially tough season for this tiny bird, which weighs about the same as just two pennies. To survive, it feeds constantly throughout the day, at about one peck per second. Every evening it huddles with others in a small group, together conserving as much heat as possible. Kinglets also tuck their heads into their feathers to further reduce heat loss through their bills and eyes.

American Tree Sparrow

The American tree sparrow flits in small flocks through snowy yards during the wintertime, pecking at the ground in search of seeds while twittering softly with its flockmates. Toward winter's end, as the snow begins to melt, these small but hardy birds will sing in bell-like *tinks* as they begin their migration back to their breeding grounds.

Downy Woodpecker

The downy woodpecker spends most of the winter inside tree holes, venturing out only as long as needed to find its next meal. But at the first sign that spring is on its way, it becomes much more visible. It's time to get to work! There are insects to collect and new homes to build. Watch for woodpecker pairs—or singletons calling for mates—while they peck away at dead branches, hammer against bark, and drill into tree trunks.

Northern Cardinal

To many, the northern cardinal represents endurance and strength. That's because these birds can survive brutally cold winters without changing much about where they live or how they look. As winter comes to a close, cardinals come together in pairs and make loud calls. Their bright red plumage and flutelike songs make them a favorite first sign that spring is right around the corner.

Dear reader,

Aren't snow birds remarkable? Before writing this book, I'd never given much thought to birds that don't migrate to warm places during the winter season. But then one day I began to wonder about these little warriors.

What I learned was that even the smallest and most vulnerable of creatures can survive anything—even subfreezing temperatures!—if they work with clever minds, keen senses, and a clear understanding of resources and conservation.

Each of the birds celebrated in this book has its own set of adaptations and behaviors that help it to survive winter's challenges. But, differences aside, *all* of the snow birds you've read about here are incredible survivors. I've paid tribute to each of these unsung heroes with its own poem. I hope you enjoyed them.

Furthermore, I hope that going forward you'll think more about snow birds. I know I will! In a world wrestling with climate change, birds are in danger of losing their familiar home ranges and habitats. The kinds of upheaval they face could be great. Let's pay attention and think about ways we can help.

Yours in curiosity, care, and birdsong,
Kirsten

For Emma and Jenni, my partners in flight!
And for Anders and Stefan, my own little warriors.
—K. H.

For my brother, Dom, who has always loved snow.
—J. D.

The illustrations in this book were made with watercolor, acrylic, pencil crayons, ink, drypoint printmaking, and Photoshop.

Special thanks to New York City Audubon for sharing its expertise.

Cataloging-in-Publication Data has been applied for and may be obtained from the Library of Congress.

ISBN 978-1-4197-4203-3

Text copyright © 2020 Kirsten Hall
Illustrations copyright © 2020 Jenni Desmond
Book design by Jade Rector

Printed and bound in China
10 9 8 7 6 5 4 3 2

Abrams Books for Young Readers are available at special discounts when purchased in quantity for premiums and promotions as well as fundraising or educational use. Special editions can also be created to specification. For details, contact specialsales@abramsbooks.com or the address below.

Abrams® is a registered trademark of Harry N. Abrams, Inc.

ABRAMS The Art of Books
195 Broadway, New York, NY 10007
abramsbooks.com